Anthology for Hearing Rhythm and Meter

This full-score anthology for *Hearing Rhythm and Meter: Analyzing Metrical Consonance and Dissonance in Common-Practice Period Music* supports the textbook of the same name, the first book to present a comprehensive course text on advanced analysis of rhythm and meter. From the Baroque to the Romantic era, *Hearing Rhythm and Meter* emphasizes listening, enabling students to recognize meters and metrical dissonances by type both with and without the score. Found here are masterworks carefully chosen as the ideal context for the presentation of foundational concepts.

Matthew Santa is Professor of Music Theory and Chair of the Music Theory and Composition Area at the Texas Tech University School of Music.

9780815391760

T0378001

Anthology
for
Hearing Rhythm and Meter

Analyzing Metrical Consonance and Dissonance in Common-Practice Period Music

Matthew Santa

Routledge
Taylor & Francis Group

NEW YORK AND LONDON

First published 2020
by Routledge
52 Vanderbilt Avenue, New York, NY 10017

and by Routledge
2 Park Square, Milton Park, Abingdon, Oxon, OX14 4RN

Routledge is an imprint of the Taylor & Francis Group, an informa business

Library of Congress Cataloging-in-Publication Data
Names: Santa, Matthew, author. | Santa, Matthew. Hearing
    rhythm and meter.
Title: Anthology for Hearing rhythm and meter : analyzing metrical
    consonance and dissonance in common-practice period music /
    Matthew Santa.
Description: New York ; London : Routledge, 2019.
Identifiers: LCCN 2019020407 (print) | LCCN 2019022267 (ebook) |
    ISBN 9780815391760 (pbk.)
Subjects: LCSH: Musical meter and rhythm.
Classification: LCC MT42 .S26 2019 Suppl. (print) | LCC MT42
    (ebook) | DDC 781.2/209—dc23
LC record available at https://lccn.loc.gov/2019020407
LC ebook record available at https://lccn.loc.gov/2019022267

ISBN: 978-0-367-34924-0 (hbk)
ISBN: 978-0-8153-9176-0 (pbk)
ISBN: 978-1-351-20083-7 (ebk)

Typeset in Adobe Calson Pro
by Apex CoVantage, LLC

Visit the eResources: www.routledge.com/9780815384489

Contents

Contents

Two-Part Inventions (1723)
No. 13 in A Minor

Johann Sebastian Bach
(1685-1750)

Fugue in B Major (1722)
From *The Well-Tempered Clavier*, Book I

Johann Sebastian Bach
(1685-1750)

Partita in C Minor, BWV 826 (1726)
Sarabande

Johann Sebastian Bach
(1685-1750)

Piano Sonata No. 1 in F Minor, Op. 2, No. 1 (1795)
First Movement

Ludwig van Beethoven
(1770-1827)

Symphony No. 3 in E-Flat Major
First Movement

Ludwig van Beethoven
(1770-1827)

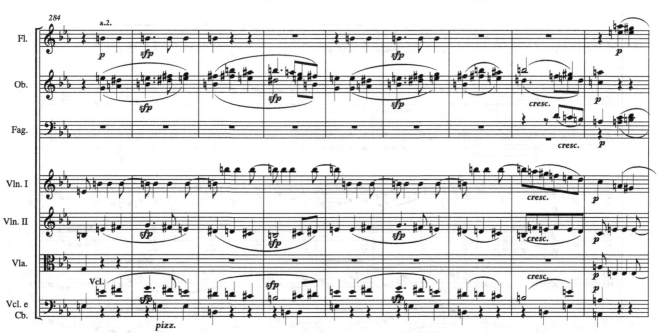

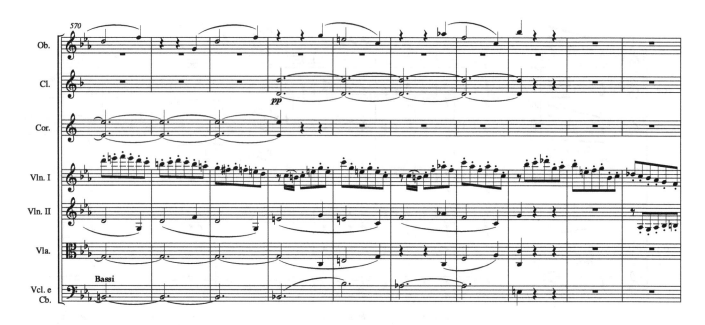

Symphony No. 7 in A Major (1812)
Scherzo from Third Movement

Ludwig van Beethoven
(1770-1827)

Symphony No. 9 in D Minor (1824)
Scherzo from Second Movement

Ludwig van Beethoven
(1770-1827)

Variations on a Theme by Joseph Haydn
Op. 56a (1873)

Chorale St. Antoni

Johannes Brahms
(1833-1897)

Var. I

Poco piú animato

Poco piú animato

Var. II

Piú vivace

Piú vivace

Var. III

Var. V

Vivace

Var. VI

Finale

Symphony No. 4 in E Minor (1885)
Fourth Movement

Johannes Brahms
(1833-1897)

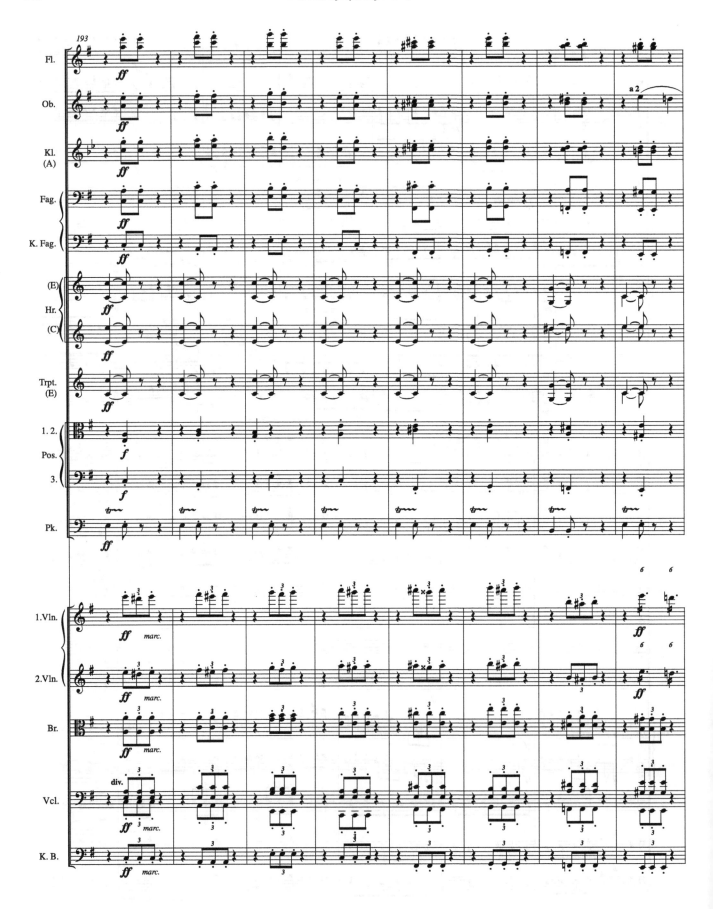

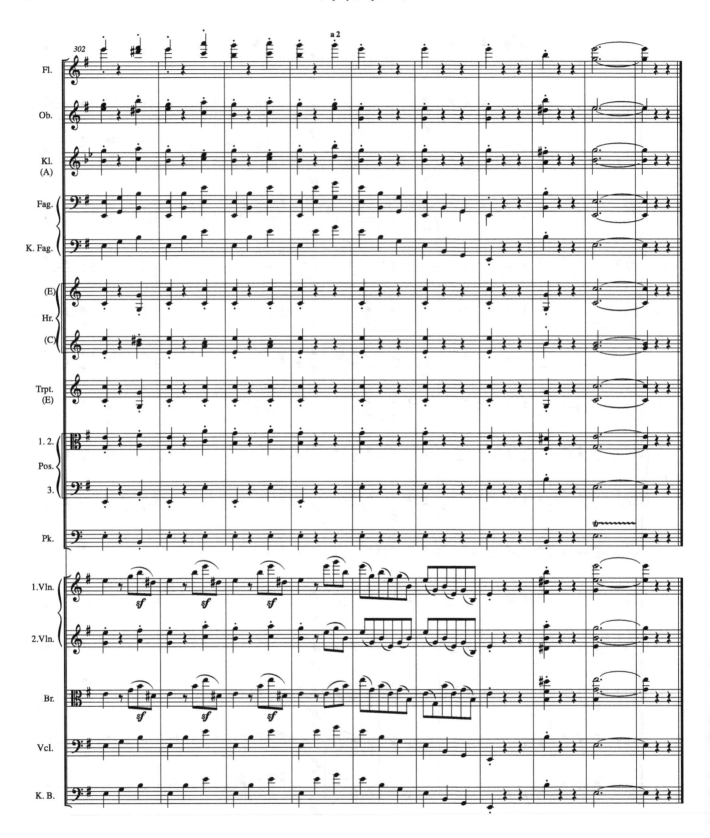

"L'empio, sleale, indegno"
From *Giulio Cesare* (1724), Act 1, Scene 6

George Frederic Handel
(1685-1759)

L'empio, sleale, indegno

L'empio, sleale, indegno	That impious, disloyal theif
Vorria rapirmi il regno,	would steal from me my throne,
E disturber cosí	and thus trouble
La pace mia.	my peacefulness.
Ma perda pur la vita,	But let him lose even his life
Prima che in me tradita	before he betrays in me
Dall'avido suo cor'	with such a greedy heart
La fede sia.	the faith therein.

Italian text by Nicola Francesco Haym
English translation by Thomas Cimarusti

Piano Sonata in C Minor, Hob. XVI: 20 (1771)
First Movement

Franz Joseph Haydn
(1732-1809)

(Allegro) Moderato

Symphony No. 101 in D Major (1794)
Fourth Movement

Franz Joseph Haydn
(1732-1809)

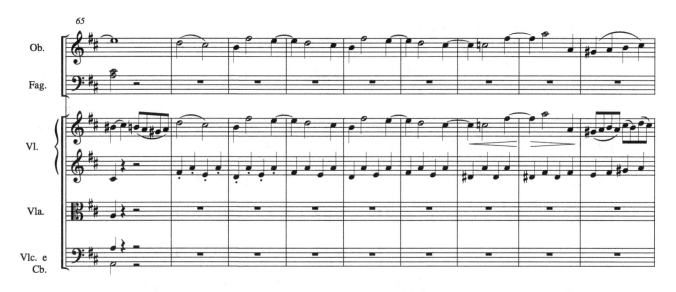

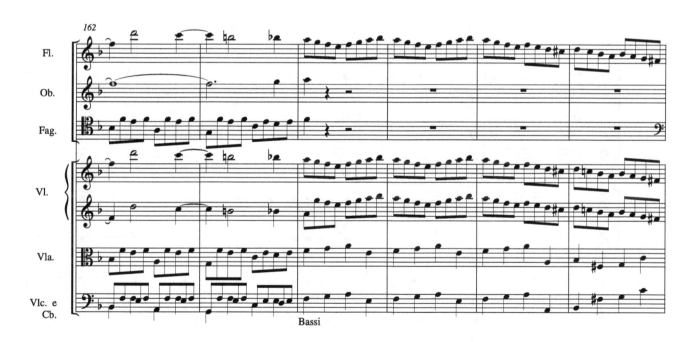

Symphony No. 103 in E-Flat Major (1795)
First Movement

Franz Joseph Haydn
(1732-1809)

Allegro con spirito

"Schwanenlied"
Op. 1, No. 1 (1st pub. 1846)

Fanny Mendelssohn Hensel
(1805-1847)
Gedicht von Heinrich Heine

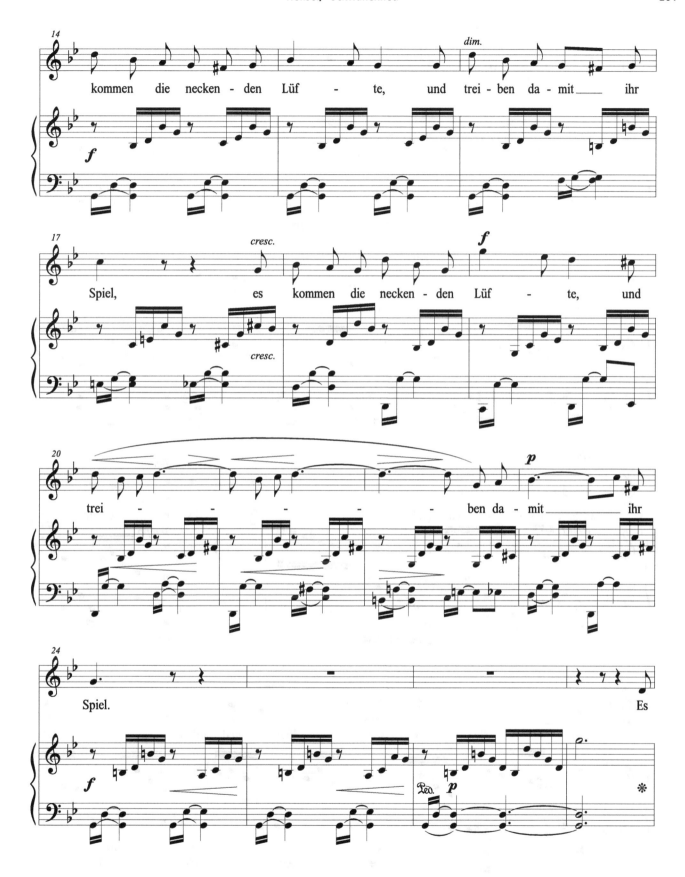

"Mayenlied"
Op. 1, No. 1 (1st pub. 1846)

Fanny Mendelssohn Hensel
(1805-1847)
Gedichte von Eichendorff

Läu - ten kaum die Mayen - glo - cken, lei - se durch ___ den lau - en

Wind, hebt ein Kna - be froh er - schrocken, aus dem Gra - se sich ge-

schwind. Schüttelt in den Blüthen - flo - cken, seine feinen blonden

Schwanenlied

Es fällt ein Stern herunter
Aus seiner funkelnden Höh;
Das ist der Stern der Liebe,
Den ich dort fallen seh.

Es fallen vom Apfelbaume,
Der [weißen]1 Blätter [so]2 viel,
Es kommen die neckenden Lüfte,
Und treiben damit ihr Spiel.

Es singt der Schwan im Weiher,
Und rudert auf und ab,
Und immer leiser singend,
Taucht er ins Flutengrab.

Es ist so still und dunkel!
Verweht ist Blatt und Blüt',
Der Stern ist knisternd zerstoben,
Verklungen das Schwanenlied.

Poetry by Heinrich Heine

Mayenlied

Läuten kaum die Maienglocken,
Leise durch den lauen Wind,
Hebt ein Knabe froh erschrocken,
Aus dem Grase sich geschwind.
Schüttelt in den Blütenflocken,
Seine feinen blonden Locken,
Schelmisch sinnend wie ein Kind.

Und nun wehen Lerchenlieder
Und es schlägt die Nachtigall,
Von den Bergen rauschend wieder
Kommt der kühle Wasserfall.
Rings im Walde bunt Gefieder,
Frühling, Frühling ist es wieder
Und ein Jauchzen überall.

Poetry by Joseph von Eichendorff

Song of the Swan

A star is falling down
From its sparkling height;
It is the star of love,
Which I see falling there.

From the apple tree fall
Many blossoms and leaves;
The teasing breezes come,
And frolic with them.

The swan sings on the pond,
And glides to and fro,
And singing ever more softly,
He plunges into the watery grave.

It is so quiet and dark!
Scattered are the leaves and blossoms,
The star has fizzled and vanished;
The song of the swan has faded away.

English translation by Yonatan Malin

May Song

No sooner do the lilies-of-the-valley ring
Softly on the mild breeze,
A youth rises with startled joy
Quickly from the grass,
In the flower petals he shakes
His fine blond locks,
Impishly musing like a child.

And now the lark songs sound
And the nightingale sings;
From the mountains the sound
Of the cool waterfall rushes again.
Around the forest are bright feathers;
Spring, it is Spring again
and there is rejoicing everywhere.

English translation by Yonatan Malin

Piano Sonata in B-Flat Major, K. 333 (1728)
Third Movement

Wolfgang Amadeus Mozart
(1756-1791)

Quintet No. 3 in C Major, K. 515
Third Movement

Wolfgang Amadeus Mozart
(1756–1791)

TRIO.

M.D.C.

Symphony No. 40 in G Minor (1788)
First Movement

Wolfgang Amadeus Mozart
(1756-1791)

Symphony No. 40 in G Minor (1788)
Third Movement, Menuetto

Wolfgang Amadeus Mozart
(1756-1791)

"Già il sole dal Gange" (1680)
From *L'honestà negli amori*, Act 1, Scene 10

Alessandro Scarlatti
(1660-1725)

Già il sole dal Gange

Già il sole dal Gange più chiaro sfavilla,   Already the sun sparkles more clearly from the Ganges,
E terge ogni stilla dell'alba che piange   It wipes off every crying drop of dawn
Già il sole dal Gange più chiaro sfavilla.   Already the sun sparkles more clearly from the Ganges.

Col raggio dorato ingemma ogni stelo,   Its rays adorn each blade of grass
e gli astri del cielo dipinge nel prato;   And paint in the meadow the stars of the sky
Col raggio dorato ingemma ogni stelo.   Its rays adorn each blade of grass.

Italian text by Domenico Filippo Contini
English translation by Thomas Cimarusti

Mignon, D. 321 (1815)
("Kennst du das Land?")

Franz Schubert
(1797-1828)

Gedicht von J. W. v. Goethe

Mignon (Kennst du das Land?)

Kennst du das Land, wo die Zitronen blühn,
Im dunkeln Laub die Gold-Orangen glühn,
Ein sanfter Wind vom blauen Himmel weht,
Die Myrte still und hoch der Lorbeer steht?
Kennst du es wohl?
Dahin! dahin
Möcht ich mit dir, o mein Geliebter, ziehn.

Kennst du das Haus? Auf Säulen ruht sein Dach.
Es glänzt der Saal, es schimmert das Gemach,
Und Marmorbilder stehn und sehn mich an:
Was hat man dir, du armes Kind, getan?
Kennst du es wohl?
Dahin! dahin
Möcht ich mit dir, o mein Beschützer, ziehn.

Kennst du den Berg und seinen Wolkensteg?
Das Maultier sucht im Nebel seinen Weg;
In Höhlen wohnt der Drachen alte Brut;
Es stürzt der Fels und über ihn die Flut!
Kennst du ihn wohl?
Dahin! dahin
Geht unser Weg! O Vater, laß uns ziehn!

Poetry by J. W. Goethe

Mignon (Do You Know the Land?)

Do you know the land where the lemons blossom,
In dark foliage the golden oranges glow,
A gentle breeze from blue skies blows,
The myrtle stands still and high the laurel?
Do you know it well?
Thither! Thither
I want to journey with you, my beloved.

Do you know the house? On columns rests its roof.
The hall sparkles, shining is the chamber,
And marble statues stand and look at me:
What have they done to you, my poor child?
Do you know it well?
Thither! Thither
I want to journey with you, my protector.

Do you know the mountain and its cloudy path?
The mule seeks its way in the mists,
In caves dwells the dragons' ancient brood;
The bluff tumbles and over it the flood!
Do you know it well?
Thither! Thither
Our path leads! O father, let us journey!

English translation by Sigrun Heinzelmann

Eusebius (1835)
From *Carnaval*, Op. 9

Robert Schumann
(1810-1856)

String Quartet Op. 41, No. 1
First Movement

Robert Schumann
(1810-1856)

String Quartet Op. 41, No. 2
Second Movement

Robert Schumann
(1810-1856)

"Morgen" (1894)
From Op. 27, No. 4

Richard Strauss
(1864-1949)

Morgen

Und morgen wird die Sonne wieder scheinen
und auf dem Wege, den ich gehen werde, wird
uns, die Glücklichen sie wieder einen inmitten
dieser sonnenatmenden Erde. . .

und zu dem Strand, dem weiten, wogenblauen,
werden wir still und langsam niedersteigen,
stumm werden wir uns in die Augen schauen,
und auf uns sinkt des Glückes stummes
Schweigen. . .

John Henry Mackay
(6 February 1864–16 May 1933)

Tomorrow

And tomorrow the sun will shine again
and on the path (that) I will walk
she will again unite us, the happy ones,
amidst this sun-breathing earth. . .

and to the beach, wide [and] wave-blue,
we will descend quietly and slowly,
silently we will look into each other's eyes,
and upon us [will]* settle happiness's mute stillness.

* Comment: In the last line Mackay changes from the future to the present tense, perhaps as if the protagonist is picturing the scene so intensely that it appears to be happening in the present.

Verborgenheit

Laß, o Welt, o laß mich sein!
Locket nicht mit Liebesgaben,
Laßt dies Herz alleine haben
Seine Wonne, seine Pein!

Was ich traure, weiß ich nicht,
Es ist unbekanntes Wehe;
Immerdar durch Tränen sehe
Ich der Sonne liebes Licht.

Oft bin ich mir kaum bewußt,
Und die helle Freude zücket
Durch die Schwere, [die] mich drücket,
Wonniglich in meiner Brust.

Laß, o Welt, o laß mich sein!
Locket nicht mit Liebesgaben,
Laßt dies Herz alleine haben
Seine Wonne, seine Pein!

Eduard Friedrich Mörike
(8 September 1804–4 June 1875)

English translations by Sigrun Heinzelmann

Secrecy

Let, oh world, let me be!
Don't tempt [me] with gifts of love,
Let this heart have to itself
Its bliss, its pain!

What I mourn, I don't know,
It is an unknown ache;
Perpetually through tears I see
The sun's dear light.

Often I am barely aware of myself
And bright joy penetrates
(through) the heaviness that burdens me
and blissfully [fills] my breast.

Let, oh world, let me be!
Don't tempt [me] with gifts of love,
Let this heart alone have
Its bliss, its pain!

"Verborgenheit" (1888)

Hugo Wolf (1860-1903)

text: Eduard Mörike